T0195665

Time
QUEST

ALBERT CERECEDES

BALBOA.PRESS
A DIVISION OF HAY HOUSE

Balboa Press books may be ordered through booksellers or by contacting:

Balboa Press
A Division of Hay House
1663 Liberty Drive
Bloomington, IN 47403
www.balboapress.com
844-682-1282

Print information available on the last page.

ISBN: 978-1-9822-7286-9 (sc)
ISBN: 978-1-9822-7287-6 (e)

Balboa Press rev. date: 09/21/2021

POEM

Rainbows

Today, I saw two rainbows in the sky. It was meant to behold—as wonders of nature and to marvel at the natural phenomena of creation. Was that the Lord's way of telling me to look to the heavens as the rainbows danced and intertwined in the sky? A reminder of the magnificence of our own existence? Two arms to hold- two ears to hear- two eyes to see- two legs to walk to the ones we love- where two hearts will beat as one. My friends walked side by side like a band of rainbows in the sky, our colors just as warm and clear as the prism in the sky. Friends beneath the rainbow's end, where the colors of the rainbow-stained pure spirits with God's delight to see two rainbows in the sky.

CONTENTS

PREFACE

It's not every day we talk about our life existence, but I felt a need to write about my time quest. We all have a message and a story to tell, some with creativity and a message that seems to come straight from our creator, others who have done wonderful things in life but never say a word.

For me, my words simply try to speak from the heart. It's like medicine to me. The words are my caretaker, and you are my healer. I hope, in time, you will read this and accept me for who I am—a man with many imperfections, searching for a reason in one's life, trying my best to be creative, putting my feelings into words and verse and poetry. A story of life's mistakes.

Lift up your heart. Make it light and see the morning the way you want. Make it your own. Call it your day. It is your day, you know. Let's make ourselves a promise here and now to make a difference in one life, to share this life we have been given.

If we step back and look into ourselves, I wonder if you're hurting too. We can find the magic and the miracles. Climb the mountains that surround us and sing to the heavens to come and share their love, the love we have never seen. Together, we can hold on to that thread of our universe and find a way to make something from nothing. We can build a home where the stars are the night lights, and the sun is our warmth and a moon to blanket us like the ocean waves. And if there ever was a day like this, you should know it belongs to you.

Let me write this story of my time quest in the hope that it will be no different from the story of your journey in time.

CHAPTER 1

My Addiction—Get Better or Die!

I'm a writer. I'm a poet. I'm a singer, musician, a laborer, a roofer. I'm a landscaper, an optician, and a machinist in the making. I'm all these things and more. I think if we add up a list, we'll find we are a whole lot of things. Some things we're proud of, others not so proud of. And then there are those things we just want to keep to ourselves and hope no one finds out. It's those things I want to talk about. Those things that make us less than who we think we are. Those things that make the world turn its back on us. Those things that make redemption near impossible.

I made a conscious choice to improve my inner self. You see, I am an addict. I am an alcoholic. I didn't think so until I tried to stop. Then the fun and games weren't just a Gilbert and Sullivan play in the park but a Greek tragedy. I decided to tell everyone, so that is what I did. Some knew, some sort of knew, and others hadn't a clue.

I wish I could have just stopped the day I decided to tell everyone, but it didn't work that way for me. When I first thought I could stop on my own, I couldn't. I tried getting help by telling the people at work, but there was only so much they could do. I wanted to go to rehab, but my insurance wouldn't cover it. So, I saved up the money and put myself into rehab. It was a step in the right direction for me. I was surrounded by professional people, hard-working people, and people who were just inches away from giving up their life to alcohol and drugs. We all shared a similar fate *get better and stop or die.* Some of us wished we could just die after all the suffering and pain we caused others in our life.

In rehab, I was told it was a disease. I had a disease of the mind and body. My mind was no longer in control, but my saturated body ran the show. My body, which I had fermented and pickled, was using my mind to navigate its way to its next drink and hit of crack cocaine. My mind was hopelessly misdirected, thinking I needed this to get by. It started out so innocently forty-two years ago. What started out as sociable and full of life was now a dark, lonely corner. However, quitting was still not a part of my plan. After all, my addictions had outlasted two marriages. It was still there for me every moment of the day. Who else could do that for me? Who else would be there for me and make me feel so good? *I mean, great!*

After a month and a half and six thousand dollars later, I came home, and it lasted two weeks. There was no magic pill or magic anything. I was still that same inner self who craved and yearned and searched for a false sense of euphoria, a place I learned to escape to in my own selfish house of doom. I just wasn't ready. My mind was no match for my primal physical desires. My body was going to get what it wanted—and it wanted more. Not realizing or caring that that house of doom had no doors nor windows. No one goes in, and no one comes out. Depression, desperation, suffocation, and the shallow promise that this would be my last time. It was never enough to make me leave my primal state of mind. Losing everything—my love, my job, my home, my respect, and my boys—was still not enough.

How in the world was I going to stop and be the person I wanted to be? How in the world was I going to end these cravings, this lack of self-control, and the selfishness? That's not me. I'm a soldier. I'm a warrior. I am disciplined. How was I ever going to live up to myself!

When someone would ask me, "How are you?" the answer was always, "I'm Alright." However, I was dying inside, and the lie was killing me. It was honesty I had to keep by my side. Honesty, like an old friend who knows me only too well. I've always felt honesty is like the North

Star in our hearts—no matter how lost we become; it will guide us home.

I can try and hide the truth, avoid the truth, run from the truth, lie about the truth, but in the end, it's the truth I need. There seems to be a certain comfort and empowerment in knowing one can speak the truth. However, the truth isn't always easy to say. It could mean the end of one's dignity, of one's respect, and of people believing in you. It could be the end of your credibility.

I guess that's why I felt the need to lie. So, I didn't lose another person's confidence in me, but the truth always seems to find its way to the top. I went to AA meetings, but something there just didn't feel right. It wasn't constructive for me, calling myself an alcoholic and a drug addict. After all, that was the very thing I was trying to get away from after forty-two years. At first, it felt a bit like a badge of honor, something I had earned to say.

"Hello, my name is Albert, and I am an alcoholic and a drug addict."

Somehow it just seemed to permeate that lifestyle in me. That life without meaning, that life without joy, that life without light. Night after night, it began to wear on me like an old suit. How far away could I separate myself from my darkest tragedy if I'm calling myself a tragedy?

I thought about my dear friends who had died from their addictions and the tragedy they brought upon their families. From their pain and suffering, I should have learned their message. One of my friends told me, "You can't stop being who you are." But if there is something you don't like about yourself and want to change—that was the key—wanting to change, you can do it.

Putting the mind back in control. You can do it by building dikes to change the direction of your life. My friend was a brilliant man, a Ford Scholars Program award winner. He said, "Simply put a positive in the way of a negative, and it will change your direction." Maybe simplicity is what I needed, a simple way to be and appreciate doing the simple things in life.

I think AA is good and has a meaning and a message for many. It just wasn't for me at the time. I may still go back, but I guess I just wanted to be alone. So, what was I to do? I had come to a crossroad in my life. What could make me stop? What could end these cravings? It's like the ride stopped a long time ago but I didn't want to get off. Having no money would be a good start; I wouldn't be able to buy my body's destruction. Giving up and just accepting the pain, the pain I was running from, not knowing where it would take me, just knowing I was going nowhere. Well, both these things came to be, and it's like being tossed about by an ocean wave and then slammed onto the rocks below.

It's hard for me to say when I began to change because I believe our redemption is so many things. First, my sons kind words and patience; second, the people who loved me; third, there prayers. I do believe someone is praying for me, and I believe in the promises made by Jesus Christ.

Remembering the stories of Christ being by the side of those less fortunate, I asked Him to be by my side. The path is still very lonely and dark, but I can see enough to take my next step. It just seemed like one day was then two days, and two days were then two months, and two months were four, then six, then seven, and so on. *But who's counting!* I don't think about it. The changes in my course of life don't include it. It's sort of like *"out of sight, out of mind; out of mind, out of my life."* Life has its *changement de pieds* just the same, life has its own steps. I cry through the cravings. I cry through the loneliness, but if I hold on long enough, I find tears of joy.

I believe in God the Father Almighty. He created the heavens and the earth. I believe Jesus is standing by my side and everyone else's, no matter if we believe in Him or not. Still, it's hard for me to truly believe the way I need to with total acceptance. He is with me every moment of my day, but I must make myself believe and remain conscious of His presence and seek God's grace, knowing without a single doubt that my creator will provide what is right for me.

I must believe in the miracle of Jesus Christ and accept His love for me—not sort of or sometimes but with every fiber of my being. Then I believe everything will be all right. I have always been a believer. I was raised that way, but now I think it's time to try to truly understand this faith. Take it to the limits, just like everything else. Only this time, it's a *positive*.

I was thinking back to the first time I got high. It was back in 1966, and I was in my friend's father's garage. I was just out of high school because in high school, I ran track and spent a lot of time training, but I did start to drink. My friends were the greatest. Always up with the times, they knew how to go with the flow. The unspoken initiation back then was to learn how to roll a joint with one hand, very impressive! I don't remember if I learned before I went in the army or was home on leave. It didn't really matter everyone was doing it.

It was the sign of the times, and it seemed just about everyone was getting high. I remember a Christmas party at my parents' home, where my brother brought a joint, and my mother and aunties were all in the kitchen giggling because they were smoking a joint. Drugs were not heavy back then. One joint didn't do much. A four-finger lid cost ten dollars and was gone in a day. LSD, on the other hand, was a real mind-bender. No one could take it and deny they hadn't experienced something new. We regularly took it about every six months. I found myself closer to nature and to God. We couldn't help but marvel at the earth's creations. Everything from a blade of grass to the roar of the ocean's wave was far beyond what any human could do. At best, we could try to understand.

The late sixties and early seventies were a mind-expanding experience for me, as it was for many. Everything just seemed to go together—the music, the turmoil, the protest, the war, the drugs, and the people. Young people were dying, and we were losing our friends. Drugs were more of a bonding paste, an epoxy that brought us all together. It didn't matter if you were rich or poor, black or white, an intellectual or a drop-out from the barrio. There was a time when we all felt the same pain. *"Peace, brother!"*

Soon, drugs became a civil way of life for me. I'd get up in the morning and go to work, come home, and get high. It was a natural thing with the jobs I had. That lifestyle started off so innocently. It was more the norm, and most if not all my friends got high. I always thought I was in control with the steps I was taking, except when I drank too much, which eventually became every time I'd drink.

The military became my first training ground, a nightly ritual spanning three continents and drunken soldiers from every walk of life, and the fun of experimenting was just beginning. It's amazing what abuse the body can take. When I look back on forty-two years of drugs and alcohol. Perhaps I didn't physically do too much damage trying to stay healthy, being active taking vitamins and getting plenty of rest. However, subjectively and objectively, I'll never know what those years could have brought.

If only I had stopped when the war was over. My lifestyle of drugs and alcohol did interfere with opportunities I chose to ignore. I was still social and outgoing, and that's how to meet girls, partying! I also liked music, so I sang in bands, and that added fuel to my fire.

Drinking became my first problem. It was easier to blend into social circles, but it became my biggest problem. I never drove without a twelve-pack in the car or without a plastic 7UP or Dr Pepper label to wrap around my beer. You could buy them at most liquor stores back then. *"Real smart ha!",* Thank God I never got into an accident or hurt anyone. Drinking and driving in the sixties and seventies was done with a socially primal acceptance. We just didn't think. If you got caught drinking and driving, the sentence was usually having to dump your beer out and promise never to do it again. Somehow, I still managed to rack up seven DUIs. If that were today, I'm sure I would face hefty fines and jail time. I was a drunken fool going on job interviews. I would first have two or three beers just to cut the edge. Wonder why I never got the job.

Time stops for no one, and the sixties and the seventies were gone. The eighties were upon us, to the hippy goers and the drug users, the protest was long over, but the party went on. The eighties introduced me to a new drug, one that had been reserved only the rich and famous: cocaine. Cocaine was great. It made a normally quiet, shy, not-so-confident person feel they could conqueror anything. After all, many great people did many great things on cocaine. Freud wrote a book. I wasn't writing a book though. What I now had was a complete "party pack": cocaine, blaze, and booze. That took me through the eighties and into the nineties, but mainly, I was just a weekend warrior going to work Monday through Friday and party on the weekends.

I lived a fairly normal life, met a beautiful girl, and had a beautiful son. He was my second son. My first wife left me in the seventies, mainly because of my drinking. I would sometimes start drinking on a Friday. After work, I'd buy myself a twelve-pack, jump in my car, turn on the radio, and drive a straight line for hours down the freeway. In the morning, I'd find myself behind a Denny's or a truck stop and a hundred miles away from home. I don't know why I would do that. If it was because I wanted to be alone, I got my wish. That same pattern just seemed to follow me; alcohol, drugs, and the road, always patiently waiting for me to come back and only too willing to accommodate a sick mind. I know I'm really not that much different from anyone else and everyone has a story. I dare not judge you or anyone else, and I hope you don't judge me. Not because I fear rejection or anything like that but because I don't think this is what we should be doing. If I can't at least try to tell the truth about myself, then what is left? I'm not a professional writer, and I realize I shouldn't start off so many sentences with the word "I," but I hope someone will read this and not have to wait sixty years to find out drugs and alcohol can keep you from realizing your full potential.

The year was now 2000 a new millennium and in the year 2001 the World Trade Center had been attacked and destroyed but I still managed to make a mess of my life. I didn't smoke pot as much or take those other mind-bending drugs. I didn't need to. I had found a new drug one that would bring me to my knees, then drag me across the floor and leave me skin and bones. *It was crack cocaine.*

Being the intelligent and inquisitive individual that I am, I learned something *new*: *how to destroy everything I had ever worked for in a single blow.* If I took a spoon and some baking soda and water, then added cocaine with a little fire, I could burn the soul right out of my body. I had reached my destination. Only death lay beyond. I would die a soulless husk, leaving only a tragedy for my family to remember. That wasn't me. That wasn't my mind. That was a body and a reptilian state of mind, trying to have its way.

There are so many ways we can go through life, because our mind can be so powerful and complex. I want to find the truth of my existence and remember my body is a gift from God, but my mind He has given to me, and together they will return to our creator, with the story of its time quest. I know there will come a day when I stand before our Lord and say, *"I am a sinner."*

CHAPTER 2

Now That My Cup Has Been Emptied

Now that time has given me more than I need, what do I do with the rest? Well, I can keep it to myself or give it away or rent it or sell it, but what I think I'll do is explore the depths of my life and its meaning to me. And now that my cup has been filled and emptied again, what do I do now. This time, I believe I will fill it again with heaven's grace, but how do I do that?

One day, about fifty-two years ago, when I was walking home from school, I cut between two parked cars into the middle of the street. The next thing I saw was a car right in front of me. What happened next still makes me wonder, because the next thing I knew, I was lying on the grassy part of the sidewalk. I had the sensation of someone pulling me from the collar of my shirt. That day I must have had *superhuman reflexes and flash like speed!* What else could have saved me from certain death? No doubt, I would have flown like Superman down the street for all to see. The next time I walked home from school, I remembered to look both ways.

I was saved just in time. It just wasn't my time. Time must have been on my side. I remember when I was just a child playing in the schoolyard, and our tears would flow like rivers from heaven to be different. And with just a glance, we could fall in love. Then our hearts would beat like thunder. The clear blue skies that filled our eyes, fresh as the morning dew and the flowers bloom, were the friends we kept at school, a treasure and true.

How we would wait for the month of June and our last chance to say goodbye to innocence, like the earth clinging to the sun's warmth at the end of a new day. But only time and maybe a few good ideas have remained the same; everything else fades away. What time is it, anyway, and *I'm cold!* I remember, as a child, I'd walk into church when no one was there. The church would be dark except for the light coming through the stained-glass windows. The air was cold. The pews were cold. The darkness was cold. And the alter floor, made of marble, was cold. I'd kneel and pray that one day, I could sing like Danny Thomas and the girl of my dreams would be by my side. *"A tall order to fill for a ten-year-old boy"* I remember passing out at the altar. It was after school and must have been from malnutrition, but in a dream, she came.

Song:

Soft as the night, she came to my side, saying to me, *"Love never dies, and dreams can always be real."*

Her smile was as bright as a summer day. Her face was as warm as a child at play. Her eyes were as deep as the ebony sea, and her word was a gift she gave endlessly. Saying to me, *"Love never dies, and dreams can always be real."*

From where she came-I know not. Her word was clear, a message-a tear that fell from the sky- with love by my side, shining her light, saying to me, *"Love never dies, and dreams can always be real if you believe, if you believe in you"*

What is to believe? As a young boy, I believed in everything, believed everything I was told, believed in saints and believed in sinners. I still find it hard to tell the difference. But I do believe in time, I'll find the answer. I am by no means a versed man. I never was a good reader; I learned by listening. I read my first book cover to cover when I was locked up in Mannheim, Germany. We'll talk about that at another time, because that was in another time and place. I believe my time on earth, like that of everyone else who's ever lived, is a message from our creator.

Song:

Life is old. Life is new. It's years ago, and we should know that what we do depends on you. Some will love, some will hate, some will give, and some will take. And what we do will depend on you. There is money, and there is greed. There is plenty. Still, there is need. And a child's plea: *"Don't let it be a hungry seed."* Some are saved, some are slain, some afraid, and some who gain. And what we do depends on you. Broken hearts, they live in pain. Empty souls, they feel the same. No love to gain. No love to gain to heal the pain. People try, and they survive. People cry when love has died.

There is no easy way to end the flame that love arranged. We have a savior in the sky. On this earth we pass Him bye. Disgraced and shamed, no place to lie in this devil's reign. And what we do will depend on you.

Now that my cup has been emptied, how do I refill it with God's heavenly grace? Do you think it wrong for one to tell their sins to anyone who will listen? If I told you my sins, what would you do? Would you pray for me or walk away in distain? Or are our sins something that we keep to ourselves and take to our graves in silence? Well,

I think we're all made the same way, of the same stuff, by the same creator, and I think She understands.

I recall, when I was about five or six years of age, my sister telling me I was going straight to hell for what I had done. I don't remember my reasoning, but I do remember my actions: pulling the wings off butterflies and lining them up in a row. I still wonder why I did it. Was it because caterpillars can turn into butterflies, but butterflies can't turn into caterpillars and time won't let me forget that?

> *Song:*

> A river, it flows- and the sea never sleeps.
> A storm is called rain- but who's to blame?
> This is your life- and we're but a flame.
> Please, open up your door- to see we're all the same.

> *Blue water, cool water.* The judgment is not mine- I am here to unwind- a simple tune- that's right for you. This is your life, and we're but a flame. Please, open up your door to see we're all the same.

> *Blue water, cool water.* The race is called time- and the feelings are mine. The question is why- and the answers to find.

> *Blue water, cool water.*

Adrift at sea, I would sometimes swim as far as I could to the open ocean alongside the sea turtles and curious fish. My reason for doing this was simple: to build my trust in God hoping to be protected outside my element and safe surroundings. I'd say a simple prayer to our Lord with the utmost sincerity: *"Dear God, please protect and watch over me."*

Well, I always made it back. I think God has watched over us in more ways than I can count or remember. But I do remember well, while in the military, being in isolation with a temperature of 105 degrees, going on 106. I saw a clear white cloud in front of me, and in this cloud a calm serenity and the people whom I loved most.

Then a priest came into the room, and two soldiers put me in a tub of ice. My eyes were open, but I felt nothing.

After coming home from the military after serving my time in South Korea and Germany, at a time when more than 50,000 young men and women had given their lives for our country, I felt disconnected. Disconnected, sad, and not a part of society. They rejected the war and us. I did my part. I went where the military sent me and did my best. When I came home, I met a beautiful girl.

Song:

She came to me -when I was down on my knee- and all that life had for me- was its misery. I was lonely.

> She stayed around- there was no hope
> to be found. She turned my head from
> the ground-and gave the sunshine away.
> She's lovely. Tears filled my head- all my
> days, my nights, and my bed. She gave
> her loving so free-she brought a rainbow
> to me. She's dreaming.

Please say you will never leave-say you will always stay-in times of need. Say you will always want to be-in love and harmony. Yes, I need you. And now we are one-with a child to call our own. We can face each day together. No, I'm not alone- believe me. I love you Maggie, she has since passed away.

I'll never regret being in the military. It was the opportunity of a lifetime. I never would have seen so many beautiful places in this world or have met so many wonderful people. Taking a trolley ride high above the clouds to the Eagle's Nest that sits atop the Swiss Alps, with snow-covered mountains as far as the eye can see. Watching a Shakespearian play performed on the steps of a fourteenth-century church in Schwabisch Gmund. Climbing the Tower of Pisa from the outside and looking through the bell tower at the marble church below. I could say I had the time of my life. So many wonderful things have come my way, like being there for the birth of my two sons. There's no way to express this other than it's a miracle, a blessing from above, and an endless gift in time. I can only ask my heavenly Father to fill my sons cups and mine with His grace in the name of His Son, our Lord Jesus Christ.

I feel we all share the same pattern as our heavenly Father and His Son. My boys are messengers, and they speak their minds, and my job is to guide them in a good direction. But I can only try, for they will know much more than I, thank God!

There was a time when I thought I knew. Now I'm not so sure. There are so many untruths, it's hard to see the light and what is right. I'm not talking about the truth we think about that stuff in our head, but the truth we keep in our hearts. The one that beats to life. The one that makes us all the same wonderful creation, that truth, like everything else on this beautiful planet.

Song:

Oh, Blue Flower, I'm writing you this song to take on into you- until it's time to go.

Oh, Blue Flower, you've long been in my heart- and no storm nor wind nor rain- could ever carry you away.

And the seeds of your younger- will grow much taller if you teach them this song to sing along.

Oh, Blue Flower, you spend your nights
in the cold and freezing rain- and wait for
the sun to shine.

And the seeds of your younger- will grow
much wiser- if you teach them this song
to sing along.

Oh, Blue Flower, you've long been in my
heart- and no storm nor wind nor rain
could ever carry you away.

I love you Airis and Derek.

Half-Empty Half-Full

Now that my cup, Lord Jesus, please be filled with
heaven's spiritual grace, I'd like to talk about the physical
realm of my time.

As a young boy, I would lie on the cement walkway
leading to our house. I'd lie there for hours, looking up
at the sky at night. The stars and the moon were so bright
back then.

I would gaze at the North Star. I didn't realize that
was how navigators found their way around the world. It
was 1958, and I was ten years old when my father bought
a brand-new station wagon and took us all for a ride—my
aunt, uncle, mom, and all the kids. I was lying in the back
of the station wagon, looking out the back window and
up at the stars. We were all laughing, playing, and having

fun, driving around for hours, when my mother asked my father, *"Honey do you know where we are?"*

My father, being a very physical man, said, "Sure I do!" and we drove around some more.

I looked up at the stars, and I could very clearly see the North Star. It was in the opposite direction to where it would have been at home. I knew what direction we had to go in, but I didn't say anything. I kind of liked the ride. My father finally asked for directions, and we headed toward the North Star.

The stars weren't the only thing I'd look at. I would stare at the sun. I don't know why I didn't go blind. But I thought if I stared at the sun, it would make my eyes brighter, like my brother and sisters. They all had blue and green eyes, whereas- mine were brown. My sister would always tell me I was adopted because my skin was darker, and I had brown eyes. That was one way to make me cry.

> *Verse:* I'm on my way to a brand-new day. I see the morning sun- and all around the sun- I see endless tides and ocean waves reaching out to the open skies. I'm on my way to a brand-new day, where the mornings dew will come- to embrace a new you.

What makes a child hurt another child? I think it starts in the home. If a child is hit enough, they will learn to hit back. If a child is picked on enough, they will learn no self-worth. I remember banging a kid's head against the asphalt in the playground, pushing another boy down a flight of stairs, and kicking yet another child. Does the violence ever leave us? I'm saddened by what I did. It was never out of anger. It was something else, something more in the way of self-defense. Like being the center on our high school football team and pulling little tricks on the defensive linemen who were trying to get our quarterback. Sometimes I'd let them pass me by, then catch their foot with my foot and flick them in the air—lots of fun. Being physical is fun; being violent is not. Basic training in the army learning how to kill, was fun. Sending our boys and girls overseas to kill or be killed was not. I was lucky no harm came to me.

Like the crazy time my best friend and I went to TJ, a bad idea from the start. We tried to siphon gas from rental trucks and nearly got shot by the security guard. Then getting drunk on the way to TJ, having no money, and ordering food from a taco stand, thinking we could grab the food and run. Bad idea. They surrounded me and slapped me to the ground. That's when my military training came in handy. I took off like a rocket from the prone position. Never got the food and had to walk home from TJ. My friend was long gone.

How did my thoughts get me into so much trouble? My desires turned into temptations- then into actions-*and bingo!* I had a few problems of my own.

I know desires are a natural thing, but it's best to keep them in check. Especially when it comes to women, our desire is probably what keeps us producing the human race. But I think there's two kinds of desire—*one that runs vertically and another that runs from left to right. One is everlasting, and the other one will kill you!*

Song:

Once in a while, someone comes along- filled with desire- lights up a fire.

Deep in your heart- a place no one has known. You want to take her in. You want to take her home.

She's all you can see. She's all you can do. She's all you can be.

Her love belongs to me. Her love is bittersweet.

Now, what could be more physical than a drive to San Diego, California? I guess physicality is the main ingredient, after all. God made us all physical to live on this earth. I'm sure there's more to follow and realms beyond we cannot even image, but for now, it was three beers and two joints, and you're in San Diego. A city of sun and bodies, made for the young and the young at heart. My days at the university were filled with life. There were people with ideas- people in motion and a kinship—not of blood or marriage but a sense of awareness- that we share the same origin. People ran together, sang together, got naked together, and where as free as human beings could be.

I pushed myself to my physical limits at times, taking a bike ride from LA to Capistrano, partying all night, then back again. Mountain climbing and repelling down dried waterfalls in the summer and camping in the snow in the winter. However, all this doesn't compare to my grandfather, a hard-working railroad man who each year would walk on his knees from home to church, about one mile each way. I was a young boy, but I remember being at church services, when everyone was watching this man on his knees, going from saint to saint in prayer. When my grandfather died at ninety-three, he had lost both his legs to cancer. In a way, I see much of my grandfather in my two sons, as well as my nephews and nieces.

Talking about my grandfather has sparked another memory. Whenever we do an act for God, we should never talk about it, because it would be like taking it from God and giving it to ourselves. Since I am now talking about my life and time, I hope God will accept my gift. Because for seventeen years, beginning in 1973, I would fast for three or four days, starting on Ash Wednesday, eating nothing and drinking only clear blue water. I started this after seeing a man having himself nailed to a cross for his Easter penance. I was moved by his commitment to his faith and to his offering to our Lord. If he could do that, I could give up a couple of meals!

I think we're all looking for approval in our own way. We all want to be validated, but sometimes, we end up feeling violated. I don't know why. Maybe it's because God gave us free will and we're made in the likeness of God, and so we play God and impose our judgment on others.

I'm thankful we have prayer and the ability to forgive and be forgiven. Prior to meeting my first wife back in the seventies, I had gone through one of the most challenging times in my life. The interesting thing about it was that no one knew. It wasn't physical; it was worse than that. I was petrified with fear. It came on one day when I went to the river with a bunch of friends. The river was packed with people, and we were all partying like there was no tomorrow. The sand was scorching hot from the sun, and the river looked like an oil slick from all the boats in the water. Then this feeling overwhelmed me. I saw the hand of Satan in everything, and the more I tried to ignore it, the worse it got.

I came home from the river, and the feeling only grew worse. I've never in my life felt so much fear, and for so long. I was home from the military, and the country was a mess. I was also home from Germany after thirty-five days in solitary confinement, at Mannheim Penitentiary. There's more to this story, and we'll talk about that later, but at the time, I was sleeping in my parents' basement. Every night, it felt as if I were sleeping in my tomb. I prayed and prayed and prayed. I don't remember when that overwhelming fear left me, but it was soon after that I met Maggie.

I think I need to learn to appreciate all the good that has come my way and remember to be humble. God wants us that way: to be humble, physical, and spiritual. Amen.

At Mannheim penitentiary the cell I lived in for a month and a half was narrow and long. If I extended my arms, I could touch both walls. The cell was long, very long, and there were bars and a small window that I could reach. If I put the chair on top of the table, climbed up on the back of the chair, and jumped up about a foot, I could hang from the bars and catch a glimpse outside, hoping the guards didn't see me. When they did, they were nice about it. They would just point their rifles at me and say a bunch of stuff in German. I took it that it meant to get down. But there were times I could see over the prison walls, and it looked so serene and beautiful. Often, there would be this girl sitting under a tree by the stream, which seemed to flow right beneath her feet. She would always have a sketchpad with her, and I remember thinking, *she must be drawing me.* I would hang with one arm and wave with the other. Now that I think about it, I'm sure there were about a hundred other monkeys doing the same thing!

You may be wondering what got me into this prison. Well, I like to think of it as brotherly love. At the time, I was touring with a Czechoslovakian band called *Prague Revival*. They were a talented group of musicians claiming asylum in Switzerland from the Russian invasion of their country. I met them at a USO show at our compound in Zuffenhausen, Germany, and their music just knocked me out. They played there for a month. I asked if I could get up and sing with them one night, and after that, they invited me up every time I was there. We all became friends and just as I was about to be discharged from my military service. The band was going to Switzerland to play, and they asked me if I would like to join them. Of course, I said yes! I got a *European out* from the military that means one ends his military service and becomes a civilian in Europe. I met the band in Zurich, Switzerland. We played Zurich, Basil, Sion, and a few places in-between before circling around to Munich, Germany. When we got to Munich, I called some friends from my old base to come and hear us play. I was looking forward to seeing them again.

One of my friends brought me a letter from home that was sent to the base. It was from my brothers-in-arms. We had joined the army together, four of us. That is probably what saved my life.

They were all coming to Germany partly to see me for a reunion, but two of them also had a *"money-making idea."* They wanted to export two thousand dollars' worth of hashish at a nickel a gram, ship it home, and sell it for fifteen dollars a gram. I was excited to have gotten the letter. I hadn't seen the boys in a long time. So, I left Munich and the band and went to Heidelberg to see my friends. The time was great. We told our stories and described the places we had been and slept outdoors along the Nectar River.

We did have a room, but Mike brought his girlfriend, so they stayed there, and it would also be a place they could do their business. As life has it, it rained one night, and we were all partying at a club and met some people who offered to let us sleep in their hallway and stay out of the rain. That was great until around four in the morning, when I was woken up with a .45 pistol to my head.

It was the German police. They lined everyone up against the walls, and there I stood for about three hours. My hands were numb. It turned out the house we were in was filled with drugs, all three stories of it, everything you could imagine. It turned out to be the largest drug bust in Heidelberg's history. And the house was full of American deserters, bless their souls. The good thing is it made all the news, and my friend's connection heard about it and tossed our mere 40,000 grams of black opiated hashish into the Nectar River—or so he said. In any event, we weren't going back to get it.

The interrogations lasted hours, but I had just gotten out of intelligence and was somewhat familiar with their methods. So, I decided to say nothing, because nothing from nothing leaves nothing. We were told we would be facing twenty-five years, but I thought I was innocent. *"Yeah, right!"*- in truth I was simply young and naive. However, we were able to get one of the best attorneys in Germany, and we also got help from the American embassy and the army intelligent division and our congressman here in California. We all made it home. We don't see much of each other anymore, but when we do, it's as if we never missed a day.

> *Song:*
>
> Pick up the losers- pick up the boozers-
> pick up the fortune- and sisters' abortion.
> Pick up the hype- pick up the fight-and
> let it all run through.
>
> Don't look back on the things you do,
> for they will surely come following you.
> Just let it all run through. Let it all run
> through.

"When we proclaim to be good, we're probably not. When we claim to be bad, we probably are. They're both blessed, the good one for trying and the bad one for being honest".

To my two young sons, I can only try to guide you along your way. Each step you take is a place I've never been. Every mountain you climb is a place I've never seen. Unanswered questions are forever passed down from father to son. Your strength, I know, will come from within. And if you ever find yourself alone, you can hold on to one loving memory. *Never stop learning, and God will light your way.*

Song:

There is a new way of life, there is a new way of being.

It's called living. It's called believing.

And believing is the answer, and the question to our life is with the universe. We are the universe. It lives inside us and all that is to infinity. I was searching for an answer to my existence when I found it at the video store.

CHAPTER 3

Looking for Salvation

There was some truth and belief in what I saw and heard. I have heard it before but never really internalized it. This is what I heard: The laws of the universe are shared equally among us. Some just know how to use it better than others.

Jesus told us about this, but I guess I just didn't understand the magnitude of His words. And many, if not all, the great people who ever lived knew this. *"Ask believing and you shall receive."*

We are God's foremost creation in the universe, and if we align ourselves with the laws and principles of the universe, we will *create* what we are asking. It happens all the time, every day. Most of us just don't know the power God has given all of us. For some reason, we look to God only for our spiritual well-being but for our daily living, our food, our shelter, and our very survival. We sometimes look elsewhere. There are those who know the principles of the universe and physically attract what they want or need through their thoughts. This is what one must do for it to work for you.

However, having millions and good health, truly a blessing in itself, doesn't guarantee my salvation. I'm sure there will come a time when everyone will know the principles and laws of the universe and align themselves, and there will be no more poverty or hunger because God made plenty on earth for everyone.

Jesus wants us to follow Him from this existence to our next, and He told us He is preparing a place for us to live with Him, our creator, for eternity, and how cool is that! *"If we are here now, we will be there then".*

The more I search, the more I find, and I thank you for letting me express myself. The more I realize we are not only a part of everything; we are everything. The air we breathe, the water we drink, the sun that fills our earth, the moon and the stars at night, the dirt we stand on everything is made of the same stuff and not a single particle out of place. So, when we think of something, our thoughts can be pure energy, tremendous energy.

There are those who have learned how to use and control their thoughts. We call them *great people.* I can only wonder where this uncharted birthright of man will take us when everyone is great! I think it starts with forgiving ourselves and others and thanking God, our creator, the creator of everything, just to know we have been given this gift of life to share. And the power to give back is overwhelming bliss.

Now that I've entered this quest to fill my cup with God's heavenly grace, I have become more mindful of my presence and that of others. It seems our thoughts are the key to existence, and everything in the universe is safely locked away in a little black box we call our mind.

Mindfulness, mindfulness, mindfulness.

This is a major requirement to be aware. If I am walking, I tell myself *I'm walking.* If I'm talking, I tell myself *I'm talking.* If I'm looking and listening to someone, then that is what I'm doing. I tell myself that is- *what I'm doing.* It's not something new. It's something we all do, and why? I think it's because it helps to keep us in the present and in *His Presence.*

The next thing I'm being led to is my five senses: touch, sight, hearing, taste, and smell. If I suppress my senses, would I become less than an animal- *a rock!* And what about my feelings and emotions? Is it possible to deaden my senses yet strengthen the rest of me? *Then what would I be?* I started writing this because I needed to find myself a better way of being. I didn't like the way I was— not that I was a bad person; at least I didn't think so—but

I had to do something. I was killing myself with drugs and alcohol, and no one was going to change for me. The world wasn't going to reverse its course for me. I needed to learn what governs my world and what governs me.

I know I exist because I'm writing these words, and I feel good and thankful, but at the same time, I feel saddened and in need of forgiveness. Please forgive me, Lord. It's not easy living, because there are so many obstacles and so many minds and so many thoughts. Yesterday, I walked to the store, but on the way back, I was tired and didn't want to walk anymore, but there was no other way to get home unless someone stopped and picked me up, but that wasn't going to happen.

Then this thought came to me. I was eventually going to make it home, but I had to physically take the next step, one step at a time, one step in front of the other, until I made it home. And so, I think that *is* the way of life. If we physically take the steps toward our goal, we will be guided no matter how impossible it may seem.

I believe the power of God is the power of the universe, and He has given us earth to care for until Jesus returns to claim it. I'm sure a billion other galaxies share our same existence. It's His tremendous love for us. I hope I have the strength and wisdom to understand this marvelous gift of life, and I hope there are many more steps to be taken. I find it awakening to make a life for myself, without *thoughtlessness.*

This morning, I went on a pilgrimage, something new I've been doing- walking to church on Sunday's. It's kind of fun. This Sunday was a bit special because the next day, I started a new job. I needed a job and one that didn't interfere with my machinist training. I went to school from seven-thirty in the morning until noon. I had to work, but I didn't want to end my pursuit to be a machinist, which required learning. I believed I could use that knowledge in the future. I was asking God, the angels in heaven, the universe, and I guess anyone else who would listen. I needed work. I had taken a break with my morning class and called a job lead that I had. I had left two previous messages, but this time, I got a real person on the line. I told him who I was and who I had been referred to by. I was feeling a bit hopeful. He said, "We don't have an opening at this time, but try again later. Things do change."

My heart felt heavy. It was Wednesday, and Thursday would be Thanksgiving. I went back to class and worked quietly on some metal pieces. When class was over only about an hour and a half later, I went back to my car, and there was a message on my phone. It was from a lab I had applied to two months earlier and was told the position had been filled, but this was another opening, and the hours were perfect for me: four-thirty in the afternoon until midnight, with raises every thirty days, based on performance.

I was ready! I was going through something I'd never experienced. My tears of sorrow turned into tears of joy.

It's funny; they both felt the same, with one exception: *elation.*

On my early morning walk to church, I was thinking, *I'm going to need gas money for Monday morning.* I looked down, and what did I see on the ground: a shiny new penny. The penny took me back to my young days with my father, how we would drive from market to market, collecting all the potato and onion sacks. There were no supermarkets back then. I would stack the sacks outside in front of the store, and my father would give me a penny for each sack. I don't think I ever really thanked my father for all he did for me. He taught me a lot, and I'm grateful for all of it. I would lay out five hundred burlap sacks and put them in a baler, then wire them up and stack them twenty feet high. There is a way of doing it. It's kind of like building a pyramid. Then I'd go with my father to the docks and watch him load the bales on the ocean freighters. The one I liked the most was the Golden Bear. It came all the way from China and had Chinese writing on the side. It looked so powerful.

My father was a very good man. He helped so many people, and I'm grateful for all he did. I miss him. He was my mother's *Superman*—I remember reading that in their high school yearbook. My father never finished high school. Instead, he went to work. He was the eldest of thirteen children in his family. And the beautiful girl he fell I love with was an orphan.

By the age of twelve, my mother had lost her two brothers, her sister, and her mom and dad. My mom *did* have a younger brother and sister that my father helped along the way. I never had a chance to know my mother's mom and dad or my uncles and aunt that passed away, but I believe there's more to our existence than what we see. My quest to fill my cup with God's heavenly grace, or at least try, has left me appreciating all the wonderful people I know and grateful for all I have received. I must go to sleep now to get rest for a new day.

Good night. I love you, and sweet dreams.

One week later …

Maintaining good thoughts and a positive disposition can be draining at times. Trying to forgive others is difficult as well.

A few weeks ago, someone had fired a pellet gun and took out the back window of my car. I live on a busy corner, and my car was parked at the end of the street, near the stop sign. There are always lots of kids coming down from Turnbull Canyon partying on Saturday nights—who knows—but my window *is* gone. I fixed it with Plexiglas. It looks all right, until I can get the money for a new one. That's not the only thing that upsets me. I'm going to school to learn machining. I really like it, but one of my instructors seems to be a bit of a bigot. You see what I mean? I'm judging someone, and I don't really want to. His actions aren't directed toward me but to another student; however, it still gets to me. Also, when I turn on the TV, so many things make me feel anxious, with all the commercials and problems. I don't know why I even turn it on!

Today is Sunday. I got up this morning and walked to church.

My thoughts were scattered, and I felt so alone, depressed, and out of place—so meaningless. My quest to understand this life seemed stupid and pointless, but I didn't want to give up. I've got to live anyway, right? Well, I made it to church, and when I got there, the church was dark and empty, except for three other people and myself. What overcame me was the scent of myrrh. It reminded me of my young days in church. It was seven-thirty in the morning, and services started at eight. Slowly the church began to fill up, and the choir began to set up. I enjoy listening to the gospel and what the priest has to say. I always look for a message that I can take with me. Today's services were in Spanish, so I wasn't sure what I would take with me, but I still wanted to hear the choir sing. What happened next overwhelmed me. The choir began to sing in Spanish, but what I heard sound like English. The song they were singing repeated over and over:

> *God enters through an open door,*
> *God enters through an open door.*

Those words were exactly what I needed to hear—for me to open my mind and heart and keep my thoughts free of judgment. Trust that the Lord will guide my way and my heart to a better place. *My love isn't perfect, but God's love is.* I must remember, God loves all of us equally.

"God loves the bigot. God loves you and God loves me just the same."

Only people have different degrees of love, understanding, and compassion. That is something I must remember while going through my day, and things just don't go my way. I've got to go to work for now, but I'll be back later, okay.

Three weeks later …

Well, I have gained more knowledge in my quest for God's heavenly grace. A dear friend of mine gave me a book written by Ralph Waldo Trine. It's been around for a while, but it's new to me. The ideas are as old as life itself. It gets to the core of who we are, where we come from, and what our full potential can be. It's like we are all droplets of water from the sea. If you took a drop of water from the sea and flew it around the world, then put it back into the sea it would be in the same waters. We all share that same force that responds to our thoughts. I have yet to fully internalize all I've heard and read. I'm still seeking to find. It's a new way of life for me. However, I do believe this is the direction of my future. I want to know more of what this life is. I look around, and I see so many wonderful things, and there is so much more to learn. One thing I do know is that my time is limited. We have only so many years to complete our quest, and at this time in my existence, my quest includes this *world and you*. We are not here alone, and there have been many people before us. We all have a family tree. I know very little about my ancestors or where I come from, but nonetheless, I'm here.

I suppose if we all went back far enough, we'd find we're all related, and what a Christmas party that would be! Keeping my thoughts together has become very important to me, as well as trying to stay as healthy as I can. I love this newfound way of life. The people I see and the things I do just seem so meaningful to me. It seems to me the more I reach out, the more I can embrace- the more there is to embrace.

Song:

When I had the chance to hold you, what I did was try to scold you,

Then just walk away. Now I'll never have that day to hear what you had to say.

I never should have walked away. So many things surround us, and there are so many things about us.

I should just walk away, but my heart keeps saying no.

I just got to let you know how I feel about you, but so many things surround you.

And there's so many things about you; I just want to be there too,

To help you on your way to see you through another day. I never should have walked away.

You see you gave me something I never thought I'd see.

You gave me a reason to believe in me.

And you're more than these eyes could ever hope to see if you ever look back at me.

If there ever was a chance for me.

When I had the chance to hold you, what I did was try to scold you, then just walked away. Now I'll never have that day to hear what you had to say.

I never should have walked away.

Each of us has a soul-or spirit-or whatever you want to call it, but there is something there, and all the days of man and science proves it. I think it's the universe in us, or God, or whatever you want to call it. What really matters is we're all from the same sea. That force within us, along with our bodies, creates us and what links us all together- our body and our soul and our thoughts- *is love*. How cool can that be? Think about it! Our thoughts will bring to us what "it" is we are thinking. Now we just need to have *good thoughts*. It's the power of attraction and the principles of like attracting like.

What I think I'm trying to say is everything we've come to be has been brought about by our own thoughts. The power of God is without limits and allows us to live in our free will so why aren't we all super-rich and super-everything? I don't know that yet, but I think it has to do with *scattered thoughts*. We are like a ship at sea; we control the instruments and the rudder, and we can change our course at will. After all, we have free will.

If we can set a course, take hold of the rudder, watch the instruments, and keep ourselves healthy, I think we can all accomplish what it is we want of life, and I think we all know when we ignore the gauges. Now, all we need to do is set that course and stay on it.

James Taylor has a line in a song that is very mindful: *"I've gone ten miles and ten thousand more to go."*

My dear friend Mary also told me something just as profound. She said, "Albert, we're already here for *eternity*."

So, I believe if we follow in the footsteps of Jesus and our goodness, we will have a better eternity, and we have a choice at this time in our existence. How exciting is that! I must go to work today, but my thoughts will be on how I can make things better for others and myself. God will show me a way. Love you, and will talk to you soon …

A few weeks later …

I have a challenge before me, one to help protect myself and others from this vicious chemical known as *hydrofluoric acid*. It has already caused one employee to have his thumb amputated. The job I have is working with a very serious chemical. If two percent of your body comes in contact with it, about the size of the heel on your foot, that's enough to kill you. The *hydrofluoric acid* seeks the calcium in your bone and will penetrate and dissolve the bone. The two compounds are among the hardest to break down. My doctor said it's the most dangerous acid known to man. Unfortunately, the company I work for has taken minimal precautions to protect its employees, and everyone, including me, has gotten burned.

As I was sitting in the emergency ward, I began to think this is why God has me here—to help address this problem. I have brought their safety procedures to the forefront of their management staff. Most, if not all, of the employees that worked in this area have accepted this, but not much has been said or done to improve safety. I have thought of a better way to contain this acid, minimizing its interaction with humans. The good thing is that management also has told me they are looking into a better way. In my opinion, it doesn't matter whose idea is put into place. The important thing is that once an idea becomes a physical thing, it can only be improved upon. Think of a car or a computer or anything. Once it's made, it can only be improved. So, the more ideas that are made, the more choices we can improve upon.

A thought came to me today: everything on earth and the universe moves by the hand of God. And man can only rearrange or horde what's been given to him. I hope and pray we can fix this problem soon so I can move on to the twelfth mile with a smile. I choose to center my thoughts and ask our Lord Jesus Christ for knowledge, health, and wealth—faith, hope, and charity- and in that order.

First, knowledge- faith, so I may understand God's will.

Then, health- hope, to give me the energy to do God's will.

Then, wealth- charity, to both give me shelter from the storm and the means to help others.

And that's; *"Another tall order to fill- for a man three score."*

Sunday morning ...

I drove to church today instead of walking because I go to work tonight, and I'm on my feet for eight hours and my dogs are barking by the end of my shift. Anyway, as I was parking my car across the street from St. Mary's, there was a gentleman walking down the street with a Bible in his hand.

I could tell by the look on this man's face he was no stranger to hard times. He was dressed in a suit and carrying a leather-bound Bible with a beautiful white cross embroidered on the front. As I watched him walk down the street, I admired his ambiance of faith. And so it was with everyone in my church. When I walked in, the choir was singing, and everyone was greeting each other and bidding them peace. I was standing at the back of the church, partly because I still have this feeling of not being worthy (or as worthy). However, people did come up to me to shake my hand and bid me peace. I looked into their eyes, and I could see their genuine affection, and there was a humming sound coming from all the people reaching out to each other.

The priest was preparing the Holy Eucharist when he said these words, which I'm sure I've heard a thousand times; only today, I could feel it. The priest said, "Lord, I am not worthy to receive you, but only say the word, and my soul shall be healed."

When I looked at all the people in church, so dedicated, warm, and loving, I somehow felt sorry for Lucifer, and I wondered if he ever regretted falling away from grace and the warmth and love of God. Do you think if all the good people in the world, in prayer, asked Lucifer to ask God for forgiveness, it could be done? I'm sure God would forgive him, and what a beautiful world this would be, with everyone in harmony.

What if Lucifer asked God for forgiveness and it was granted? What would that mean to us as people? Would our thoughts then be pure? Would that then be the end to evil? Would we still be people with imperfections? Would it be the end of original sin? Would we only speak the truth without need for lies, for fear, for rejection, for acceptance, but rather just to be whom we are?

What good has evil done for us, anyway? It's the end to many Dreams and has led many astray. Perhaps, in time, our thoughts will put an end to all this, and all that mind power will connect with the positive forces of the universe. Then I believe we can truly move mountains! I also think much of our evil is our own doing. We don't need an outside force. The power of change is in us. Evil is real because our thoughts can create it, just as our thoughts can create prosperity, hope, and charity. We can also create the dark side of life from our thoughts. So, if all this is true, then our thoughts manifest all that we see and do, and I'm sure there are plenty of people doing both good and evil. After all, it's our choice. We have free will.

I thank God for coming to us in the name of Jesus Christ and giving us a path that leads us back to our creator. We have been given this miraculous and powerful gift of life. Our creator has given us a glimpse and all the attributes of being a mini-God, made in His image, if only for a mere ninety years or so. We are all part of the same pattern as our Lord. The only difference is our Lord is; all-loving, all-giving, and all-forgiving and lives for eternity.

From everything I've heard and read, at this point in our existence, we have the chance and opportunity to spend our eternity in the arms of our Creator. I hope we all find the path to make it a walk of a lifetime. Love you, sweet dreams and goodnight...

When I woke up this morning, my body ached, and I knew I had to face another day of hard work and uncertainties. I asked God for guidance and the strength to make it through the day, something I've been doing lately, while taking a shower.

My day at the machinist training center went well and I had time to come home and have lunch with my son, something we haven't done in a long time. We laughed and talked and forgot about our problems for a while. It was rejuvenating.

I was at my night job. Around ten-thirty, just before I was preparing to work with that vicious chemical, these thoughts came to me …

There were two spirits sitting at a bar. One was a lost, lonely soul in a world of hurt and on his own. And across the bar from him was this sumptuous, gorgeous bright spirit. He looked across the bar at that beautiful, beautiful spirit and thought, *Man, what is a beautiful spirit like that doing in a place like this?*

He got up and began to walk toward her. She looked at him, and with her big sky-blue eyes and angelic face, she said, "Is that your penance in your pocket, or are you just happy to see me?"

There was this beautiful lady. She read her Scriptures every night and denied her every desire. She believed one day; all her desires would be met in heaven. When she finally did die, at ninety-two, and went to heaven, she was met by the Angel Gabriel and St. Peter. As they opened the door to heaven, she ran inside and frantically looked around, then turned back to St. Peter and said, "Where's the beeef!"

St. Peter quietly replied, "Eternity is like a box of chocolates. You never know what you're going to get."

So, I believe we can only do our best and make excellence of what we have. My son Derek and I took a trip to Spokane, Washington because my eldest son,

Airis, was getting married. We really couldn't afford to go, but then again, we couldn't afford not to. He married a beautiful girl and into a wonderful, caring family. We didn't have much to give them, except our love and a song to sing.

Song: "Jenn's Wedding Song"

Dressed in white lace- pure as divine grace- she walks from her father's arm- so in love- to take the hand of her man.

Their spirits unite. In God they love. Heaven rejoice- for they made their choice- in You.

Angels sing- in harmony. All her friends are here- and the one she loves-is by her side.

Love is one-a home is too! And three will be- a family- for eternity.

We love you, Jenn. We had a wonderful time, and it was the beginning of a wonderful recovery for me. This is when I began to write about my time and recovery and what it means to me. My boys have been such an inspiration to me. They are forgiving souls, and they always see the best part of a person. I hope and pray that God will light their way. I often talk about our existence with my younger son—about who we are and what our purpose is on this earth. We often find ourselves having fun trying to find the patterns in life that repeat themselves, from the simplest to the most complex. And here is a thought. I call it the *"Big Banger theory."* No proof, no studies, just a thought. Why do you think we all strive to be number one, the first to cross that finish line? The need to conqueror and leave the rest behind. To win at any cost. Why are we in such a hurry to get there and get that parking space before someone else does, then feel great about it! A sense of accomplishment, that striving to be number one.

I asked myself: Where does that pattern come from? We all have it, but where does it come from? Well, I think it *all* began long before we can remember. We were a *tiny little sperm* in the race for our life. We are the champions of this world! I guess to say it politically correctly, we are *"Thee Sperm Heads"* we outmaneuvered, out swirled, and ran our little tails off, beating out hundreds if not thousands, and we came in first! Congratulations, you outsmarted, outwitted, and ran circles around the competition. You, my friend, *won the egg!* We are still that mighty little sperm that won the race, all grown up, and that pattern goes on and on and on. It still feels great to win!

Then I wondered: What is the pattern of our existence as a man and a woman? I think we all know what a man is—*a little mini-God*—but a woman. What is a woman? What would she be? The more I thought about it, the more I believe she holds the pattern of the universe, and the woman shows us the pattern of our world. The woman carries a child in her womb as the earth carries us in its atmosphere. The woman provides warmth, nourishment, and protection for her child. Our earth has an environment and a sun that provides warmth, nourishment, and protection for us all. We have stayed precisely 93,000,000 miles away from the sun for several hundred billion years or so. If we were any closer, we'd burn up. If we were any farther away, we would freeze to death.

If we look at the pictures of our universe, we can plainly see we are the womb of our galaxy. The other planets are just rocks, there to protect us from debris in space. We are born into this world and into another womb. The earth is a womb, and we are once again incubating. Only this time, we are watching a birth from the inside of the womb. When a woman gives birth, the afterbirth is discarded. When we die, our bodies are buried. However, there are 21 grams of us in weight that leaves and is not accounted for. What do you think that is? When I watched my mother, father, and best friends die, and when I was in hospice while others were dying, I noticed they seemed to go into a coma-like state. I somehow think it wasn't a coma state they were in but more of a labor state, much like a woman about to give birth. And the pattern repeats itself; we are born again, and I would imagine into a place just as real and physical as the one we are in now.

51

Every galaxy has a womb, or a planet, much like our earth, and there are billions of worlds, but the nearest galaxy to us is 2.5 million light years away—hard to send a message—but there I think we'll find more of God's children and that they'll be much like us.

Sooner or later, we must realize we are much too refined in body and mind, as well as every living creature on this globe, which is precisely made for its survival and reproduction, to think we are anything less than created and cared for. We physically can't travel to other galaxies, but I believe our thoughts can and we do it all the time. *"We pray to the heavens- and our prayers are answered- every day- all the time- for everyone."* Now if we can find a way to channel that energy and send it toward another galaxy. Here's a thought: How do we become a positive receptor? Well, maybe we should think of ourselves as a magnet, which has a positive pole and a negative pole. My son and I looked at some magnets the other day and were just analyzing their properties. For a magnet to exist, there needs to be a total positive pole and a total negative pole. So, how does that relate to us and our positive energy? Well, like a magnet, we need a total positive pole—that can be our heart and mind— and we also need a total negative pole for it to work. So, I started thinking, we naturally have a negative pole. When we intake food, we take the nourishment from it and discard the rest, and that area is where the negative force can stay to keep the mind and heart totally positive. Whenever negativity comes into our lives, as we know it will, send it there.

You don't want it ruining your day, anyway. Put it in its rightful place and get rid of it! That will leave your mind and heart totally positive so the principles of attraction and like attracting like can work in a person, as it does in a magnet.

Another thought: the universe God has given to us is one we must share, and the smallest acts of kindness can also be the greatest. I believe I have found a way to fill my cup with God's heavenly grace. God will bless me with everything on earth, but in return, I must return my blessings with gratitude and graciousness to others. I hope something I have said can help another person along their way on their journey's quest in time.

I've found hope to be more than a word we use when life has taken the better part of us. For me, hope means to be determined, confident, and courageous in my goals. Hope means to be determined, confident, and courageous in my belief, and hope means to be determined, confident, and courageous each day. I want to meet others on their journey's quest so I can learn what they have learned and so I might understand what they understand.

May our Lord know we are thankful for all we've been given, even though we may sometimes forget under the pressures of daily living and so many ways to be. If we could just step back and look at what we see and become, we may be able to enjoy life in its entirety. Have a good night. Sweet dreams. Love you.

Here's another thought: I know not everyone believes in God or Jesus, and maybe the things that happen to us happen because of chance and the mere fact we are alive. I just can't help feeling we're all attached to an invisible umbilical cord that stretches throughout our universe— one that holds every being who has ever lived or ever will. A living spirit without time or matter or space or light. It's another place, another dimension, and a place we all will go to. Without the affections of the world, everything here on earth is governed by gravity, except our thoughts. Maybe that is all there is, after all, it's the beginning and the end.

It sounds so simple—that part of us I'm talking about, our spirit, that part of us we can't see, touch, or hold, that transcends our being. That is why we can think it doesn't exist— because it wasn't created. It was here before our creation. Before the planets and the sun and the stars and moon, before everything was created, there was our spirit. Without time, without matter, without space, without light from the sun, there was a Presence here before creation, and that is what is in us, and that is where we return.

What was here before the big bang is also a part of us, and that spirit cannot be corrupted. It lets us know what is right. It's that voice in us that only you can hear, that speaks the truth. It's always here and always will be here. If we are truly made in the image and likeness of God, there is no doubt eternity lives in us. What could that possibly mean to me? Well, knowing that there is a part of me that has always been here and a part of me that will go on forever adds a new dimension to who I am. We should all enjoy this gift of life, these few pounds of clay we've been given that have been wrapped around this eternal spirit. And we should know we are all a part of a Master's plan who breathed *life into stone*. With all the joy, happiness, love, and freedom here for us. And we can trust it is written in our universe.

Goodnight, and sweet dreams.

CHAPTER 4

What Is Redemption?

What is redemption? It is defined as the improving or saving of something that has declined to a poor state. To be redeemed is to be saved from apparent irreversible damage. So, how is this done, and is redemption available for everyone?

What must I do? What will I be? Is it possible to redeem myself? A teacher once told our class that a wise man always looks to the ground when he walks. As I search for my own redemption, I do feel something when I look to the ground. Not that I'm a wise man, by any means. There is a sense of oneness when looking down. If I'm not looking at others, there's less chance for me to judge, envy, lust, and criticize. Now I just have to watch for cars, so I don't kill myself.

Redemption may be a private matter, one that includes only me and my Creator. It's my communicating with our Lord and my Lord communicating with me. My attempt to bring redemption into my life started and ended at the marketplace.

I went to buy a six-dollar roast for the week and saw a beautiful young lady with a child. We were both looking at the same piece of meat. What my mind wanted to do was look at her beautiful assets, for no other reason than to admire her beauty. Obviously, this would have been an act of lust on my part. I bagged my roast and walked away. I don't know if I can keep this up all day.

My next stop was the dollar store. I parked my car out front and was approached by a young girl, who asked me for some money to feed her child and herself. Although I felt it would be used to buy drugs, I gave her my change anyway and told her about the soup kitchen at Calvary Chapel. It wasn't for me to judge her, just to offer help. In the dollar store, I found what I was looking for—a box of cake mix for only a dollar. At the market, they wanted $2.79 for one, so I bought two. As I told the clerk about the price difference and what a great deal they had, the clerk accidentally gave me too much money—a dollar more. I didn't realize this until I had gotten to my car.

At that moment, I felt my effort to find redemption was being tested. If I were to improve something that had been irreparably damaged, I had to start from the inside. I went back into the store, returned the dollar to the clerk, and we both apologized for the mistake. We both said we were sorry. I don't know exactly what that means yet, but I find it interesting. I'm not financially well at this time, and I've asked for help from the ones who love me. I live for the day I can repay them for their kindness.

I went back the next day for another purchase, and I thought I certainly would be remembered by the clerk for my good deed. As I approached the counter with my items and bid the clerk a good morning, I got no response, no eye contact, not even a smile. The previous act probably held no significance to her—to be able to balance the books at the end of the day—or maybe I had embarrassed her, or maybe it just didn't mean that much. I think maintaining good thoughts, not judging others and doing what is right, is probably a good start, but the stars aren't going to fall in.

Currently, I feel it's near impossible to walk through one day without some kind of bad thought or act of selfishness. Forgiveness becomes a major key, and confession opens the door to a brand-new day. I'm learning God isn't something up in the sky. God is everything, including the sky. I think God speaks to me through everything. What I must do is try to understand His language. Forgiving others is hard but not impossible. How can I ever start anew if I can't shed the old? Once again, there is a mountain to climb, only this time, I should be on my knees if I can't forgive.

I sometimes wonder why I have the need to find the heart of my existence, and just what do I expect to find? For years, I exploited my existence. If the pressure got too much, I could escape with drugs and alcohol. But perhaps the heart of existence is right in front of me and is just to Love one another. Maybe. But I need to find a lifestyle that serves me as well as improving the lives of others. That is something Mr. John Nash, Nobel Prize winner, worked so hard to find. If I can create my own heaven here on earth, without God, then what must heaven on earth be with God? If there is a glimmer of truth and hope in being one creation, I must try to find that "something" we can all understand—if for no other reason than to add meaning to my life.

I'm going to try to make this day a good one. It is important for me to start each day with a prayer, then look for the answer. I can't help but feel there is something extraordinary about our life, more than we know. Being older now, I look at things a little differently—things that surround me and the trouble I see also on TV. There is a certain anxiety and a need for prayer—especially for our children- even before myself and my own redemption.

My son and I watched a film about St. Joan of Arc, and it made me think of abused children. Abusing children is exploiting our most precious resource and stealing our earth's future dominion. Children need to be cared for and listened to and given ideas and a strong spirit of their own. They need a patron saint to call upon for strength, and who better than St. Joan of Arc?

She was a young girl who led the French army to victory over the English and saved her country, and she did it all before the age of nineteen. She was a pure spirit led by the hand of God in the name of Jesus Christ. I couldn't help but think her message to the world was for the young to call upon that courageous spirit for guidance and strength. I think St. Joan of Arc would be a much-needed patron saint of children in today's world.

As a child, I would pray to St. Jude, the patron saint of impossible dreams and lost causes. The world we're living in today in many ways is better than it was when I was young. There are more Americans of different types enjoying more luxuries than ever before. Still, there are many uncertainties and many more grabbing for that pie. I sometimes wonder about that pie. Will it become survival of the fittest? If you snooze, you lose, and I'm not my brother's keeper! I wonder, if I go through life thinking I don't need anyone, will anyone need me? And that can't be good. I think I sometimes just get too caught up in everything and need to find a way out.

Dream …

I once had a dream. There was an emperor who ruled a small province. Everyone in this province worked for the emperor. The emperor governed with absolute power. I found myself making stringed necklaces made of rare jewels. Everyone had a booth to display their goods, and no one was allowed to leave the province. The emperor made it clear with his guards and only one vehicle that no one would leave his province.

Once a week, the emperor conducted a tour of all the booths in his little province. Everyone lined up in a row, like in a swap meet. He would walk around looking over all the creations made of gold, silver, and precious jewels. At the end of the day, the emperor would choose the pieces that pleased him most.

Not knowing how I got here, somehow, I had been cast into this province. My jeweled necklaces were good but not good enough. I wasn't chosen. The emperor chose two other subjects. He took their creations and honored them each with a shield and a gun. Then, for his pleasure and entertainment, the subjects were to duel to the death.

The shots began to ring out, first ricocheting off the shields as the crowd cheered with the emperor's delight. Then the bullets began to hit the flesh. Each subject tried to hit the other's kneecap first, then the legs, then the arms, and then the face. One subject fell to the ground as his kneecap was shot out of its socket.

I knew I had to do something. I looked around and saw the emperor's car, and while all eyes were on the duel, I ran to the emperor's car. No one would dare take the emperor's car. I jumped in, and the keys were there, so I took off. Three other subjects joined me, and we headed for the docks. The dock master was there on the phone as we approached. He had been alerted we were trying to escape. The other three subjects surrendered, but I just couldn't, so I ran to a boat docked at the levee. I set sail and broke through the first levee, and then the second. As I followed down the channel, I saw a weak spot in one of the levee's walls. I continued down the channel, only to find myself back where I started. The dock master was laughing and pointing at me, along with the emperor's guards. I remembered that weak spot in the wall and took the boat through that spot in the levee. I rammed the boat through the weak spot in the wall, falling several hundred feet to the ocean below. The boat shattered into splinters, but I found a broken plank and a Robinson-May bag that I used for a sail.

As I was heading out to sea, thinking I was free, around the corner came the emperor's guards on jet skis. They surrounded me and held me there for the captain to come. The captain looked at me, shook his head, and said to me, "You made it this far, son. Go ahead. You're free."

For some reason, I've never forgotten this dream. It was back in 1976, when I was landscaping. Some dreams just seem to stay with me, like the dream when I was sitting on a porch and this pretty blonde girl gave me a letter. The letter talked about all the good people who ever lived. It included a list of their names. Some I'd heard of, like Buddha and Mohammad, but others I did not know. At the end of this list was the name Jesus Christ and a footnote that read, "There are many good people who have lived but Jesus is the One, *Jesus is the Light of the World*. He is the One." That dream I never forgot.

I had another dream in the seventies. I was at an outdoor-church service, and in front of the altar were life-size statues of Jesus and the apostles. As I was praying in my dream, I was taken aback to see the statues on the altar come alive and walk down the aisle to the back of the church, where I was standing, now on my knees, holding on to a rock. Jesus looked at me, then turned to one of His apostles and said something in his ear. The apostle opened a box and handed me a joint.

There's another dream I never forgot. I can't explain it, and I don't know what it means. Some people do great things after having a dream. Some people write beautiful songs and foresee wonderful things. If we truly are one creation, then everything we dream, see, or do is magnificent in its making.

Obedience brings us blessings, and blessings bring us belief in both ourselves and God. God has told us our bodies are His Temples of the Holy Spirit and His love is to share, and His abundance is there for you and your children and your children's children. I must try to find my greatest potential, whatever that may be, because I have no more worldly possessions. I lost it all. Nothing to leave my children, so I must try to find a way to live- that will bring worth into my life. And my children will value what I've done, and God will bestow His blessings upon them. I don't know if there will ever be a day when we all think the same way and go in the same direction, like some worlds in time have done. But I think we can feel the same love and care for others as we care for ourselves. Perhaps only tragedies and devastations can bring us to that point, but must we wait to find that love?

CHAPTER 5

Finding a Way

It seems I'll never find a clear path to my life. Maybe it's my lack of intellect. Maybe it's where I live. Maybe I think too much.

Eckhart Tolle says in one of his books not to listen to that voice in your head so much but to get in touch with your inner physical being. That seems to be right with me, because when the blues hit, that seems to be where I go. The job I had, which I thought had come straight through spiritual intervention because it came at such a low point in my life, turned out to cause me physical damage. My fingers dislocate from the joints every time I tried to make a fist, and my arms go numb every time I go to sleep.

My doctor has become a doubting Thomas, because after taking a shower and soaking my hands in water, the numbness goes away. My positive thinking has yet to yield any positive results. Maybe it's just me sabotaging good fortune when it comes my way.

I'm not used to having a lot. I wasn't raised with a lot, but I do pray a lot, and I do ask God for guidance a lot. I'm facing some major changes in my life and feel I need spirituality in my life. I'm beginning to think our spiritual side rarely interferes with our physical side. I'm living in a physical world with physical things and physical people, and I must account to that. I'm taking what I've learned spiritually and applying it to my physical life, and that is how I can interact with the people I meet every day. I'm not going to ask God for things, then pray for them and just wait around for them to come to me. That is not going to happen. I shouldn't pray and think that things are going to happen the way I think they will. That is just my ego wanting its way. That voice in my head that tells me what I want can leave me wanting more and more, and it's never satisfied. I must find a way that defines who I am beyond all things. To be true to myself and my surroundings despite my adversaries and my own contradictions. I want to find a way to go through a day doing the right thing and benefiting from it as well, not using others or letting others use me. Not getting upset but rather recognizing the fact that most of us do talk through our egos, and we're usually self-indulging.

I'm no different from an unborn child being ripped and torn apart in an *abortion* because someone didn't want me. The only difference is I have a voice and eyes to see- and people around me- did want me and did care for me.

So, I think: What do I profit from living today, and why am I here while some were never given a chance? Have I been given the gift of life or brought here just to wage war against others who share this same gift? This world is far from a perfect place to live, but it is beautiful and abundant, with everything we need to live in balance. It provides for every living creation's nourishment and means to flourish—with one exception. We are left here to govern ourselves with what little brainpower we have been given. We all know there is no one without fault, we all know we can't read into each other's mind, and we all know that lies, deception, greed, and all those other imperfections are in every walk of life. So what do I do? Do I look at others- critical of their imperfections? Do I think I'm better than others- so they are less than I am?

Jesus said, "I criticize others and find fault in them but fail to remove the log that is in my own eye." There must be a reason for my life other than to try and make money for myself, feed myself, and make sure myself is full of myself. I am truly grateful to my sons, my family, and my friends, who have helped me in my time of need. What I need to do now is find a way to interact with people who- don't care for me- don't like me- and are unkind to me. What is my purpose with them? Are they here for the pickings- or will they pick me apart- like an *abortion*?

This life would have very little meaning if I were here just to satisfy myself. I know because I tried it, and it's fruitless. I don't know if anyone can get enough of this world to satisfy their ego. So that's not the way for me. Maybe if I find a way to love the world the right way and appreciate all that exists- I will pass to my next existence with *"abundantia semper ama- abundant love forever."* It seems we can't govern ourselves without eventually going to war. It makes me wonder if we took all the governing powers of the world and put them on the *same island*, would they fight over what has been *given them*? Trying to find the love that is within us - that breathes life into us- is somehow being taken for granted- as if it will always be here but that may not necessarily be so true. I go through my day and try to do all the things I need to do to make ends meet with my God and my world. To have no clear understanding why we can kill each other over religious differences and hide the truth- to personify an illusion of perfection. My search for heaven's grace is hardened because it's based on blind faith. Is there a secret truth to our existence that I don't know about? Maybe the necessary things are all inside me. God lives inside me. I don't need to look to someone else to wage war because they think different than I do. I just need to look inside me and be silent so I can hear *myself breathe.*

Asking God to light my way and believing Jesus wants me to live life as He did, seem that so often, Jesus is only used to sell products, and a gimmick to get to a person's psyche and control. Which makes me think there is something terribly misused and exploited- yet God does not interfere with our free will. I go to different churches during the week to see people getting in touch with their higher powers—our Lord Jesus Christ, the celestial planets, Yahweh, and Mohammad are just a few. Then I go to school and talk with friends who believe in Buddha. I see them getting in touch with a higher source, a source within them. I can't be Buddha. I can't be Jesus. But I can be myself, living through Jesus, my source.

I wonder if we put Buddha, Jesus, Mohammad, and all the other good people of this earth on the *same island*. Do you think they would find a way to live perhaps in the name of *love and purpose*?

CHAPTER 6

A Blessing in Disguise

What can make you smile? What can I possible say to brighten your day? Is there something that can be said to remind you of a cherished moment in your time? It may be easier, however, to find the pain in your life. Have you ever felt alone and misunderstood? Or have you ever said something you later regretted or done something you believed could not be redeemed? Worst yet, have you ever known you've hurt someone else needlessly! Perhaps there are more reasons for unhappiness than happiness. You do for others, live a good life, respect others, and still get nothing in return; or on the other hand, maybe you're miserable because you are selfish and only think of yourself, using others, and given nothing in return, goring yourself in righteous superiority.

From every walk of life will come a day of sorrow. It's only natural. We are left wondering: Why! Why me?

What did I do to deserve this? Why me! I tried my best. I did good to others- and still- I suffer! What must I do to be happy?

Behind every tragedy, behind every tear, behind every misfortune is a blessing in disguise. Behind everyone with a bad disposition, everyone who's made a bad decision, every misunderstood person, there is a blessing. We only need to find it- to feel it- to hear it- and see the light that surrounds us- then follow it to a brighter day. There are many paths we can take in life, but we all share that final resting place. We all have the same destiny- and the road we walk on isn't made of dirt. The path is intertwined in space and eternity. Our thoughts never touch the ground. Its gravity, electromagnetic energy, and neutrons that hold us here as we search for the meaning to our existence. Our creator awaits our return to tell the story of our time quest and the blessings we discovered in disguise. We are never alone. You can trust in that- and whatever has pulled you down will lift you up on the last day.

Remember, your love can overcome a multitude of obstacles- and the bridge we build is between our hearts and our minds. And the strength we need surrounds us with God's love and compassion that keeps building you up. So, I wait and pray quietly to myself and repent each day for my mistakes. I have no answers to anything, only my faith and hope for a brighter future. This life, I believe, is worth saving, and our creator wants us to live, love, and be happy the right way. I also believe we all know deep inside what is right and what is wrong. But I also believe what is right for some isn't right for all, and our judgment of each other is limited at best. So, what do we do? For me, I'll change my focus to express my limited time on earth and appreciate my days and be thankful for this gift, which will last me an eternity.

If I look at my life as everlasting, I see things differently. What is our journey's purpose? We entered this life with nothing, and we will die with nothing- *except for the treasures we store in heaven*. This space and time we call *today* is a message from our conscious realm, not always easy to understand. Empty pockets and desperate hands breed disparaging loss of self-purpose, and our dignity lurks in the balance. No wonder there is no *God* if that is all we can see, all we can do, all we can be. Loneliness can also make a nonbeliever out of me and give me a heavy heart, sometimes too heavy to bear. And people I meet have nothing good to say. That makes for a very long day.

If you ever find a day like this, don't despair. The world keeps turning, and hope is always there for you. When you think you've had enough and you can't take anymore, look around you, and you will be amazed to find- *there is always someone who needs a helping hand - your hand.*

CHAPTER 7

My Time Quest

My time quest has now entered its second year, and what I find is the empty space between those words and the blessings in disguise. The unapproachable, the unbelievable, and the hopeless hoping for a miracle. To speak for someone else is only a detour to the way I feel. The things I see- the things that happen to me- and the things that pass me by. What I feel and think may never come to pass- and what I feel, and think may never last- for my life is just a passing phase- but the giver of life has breathed my name *none the same*.

Maybe the physical side is all there is, but I don't think so if history, the Bible and every great nation calls on God. There is a greater spiritual side. I see an untouched world within me, one that believes in me. I see my body as a temple for this spirit, and the same God of yesterdays is the same God we have today and will have tomorrow.

We don't need another prophet. God sent us Jesus, and if we can't believe and accept Him, what good is trying to convince someone of His existence. It is my actions and way of life I need to show. What I need to do is tear down some walls in my temple, to make room for my honored guest. I should make sure to give Him the healthiest of foods and plenty of clear blue water, and make sure my house is warm and strong that can weather any storm. And I must have music and dance, for I know His Spirit will be elated to see me. I must work on my house every day in hope that the Spirit will come to stay.

Oh yeah! What is happening! I wish there was a guideline to being me, but there is none, I wish I cou8ld figure out why the number 8 is in the word "could!" I guess I will n4efver know everything to life, but I will keep tr4ying, for this is life! My progress is very slow, my days are very long and, as a machinist, very physically enduring and demanding. A challenge I accept. Nothing is easy, and there is so much to learn about this world. What makes it round and straight simultaneously? Lately, I don't seem to be connecting well with people around me. Maybe I'm too serious, too deep in senseless thoughts. Maybe it's because I'm not certain what it is I want from life or what life wants from me. I just ask Jesus to please be by my side.

I sometimes feel hopeless on my own. Don't get me wrong; I'm still that outgoing and funny guy, but I sometimes feel as if I'm on a different page. The things that matter to me seem to make no sense to others. I must find a way to be prosperous and happy in the presence of the Lord.

I went to church today, and the Gospel was about the time the Pharisee tried to trick Jesus with a question about money. They asked Jesus if we are to serve God, then why should we pay taxes to Caesar? Jesus answered, "Render to Caesar what is Caesar's, and render to God what is God's." That left me wondering: What do I render to God? What is God's? I know what Caesar wants: Caesar wants everything!

Does a rich man interrupt this any different than a poor man? If a rich man becomes a poor man, whom does he support first, his debtors or his family? How does a man who's lost everything walk in the sunshine and praise the Lord for everything *and mean it?* I can speak for that man because I've seen small miracles in a hopeless situation breathe new life into another day.

What God wants is me. He doesn't need the Seven Wonders of the World or the mountains and rivers or the trees or ocean breeze or the other creations He made. What God wants is me, *just me.* He doesn't want my house or my car or my clothes or my food or my drink or my money. All He wants is me, *just me.* That is how I can walk in the sun and face each day, thanking our Lord for every breathe I take. There are still many unanswered questions, and I don't know what tomorrow will bring, but I can try to do the right thing *now* and mean it!

Somewhere in there is a key that opens the door to the meaning of this life. This life is meant for living and giving and sharing and loving one another the right way. It just feels right to have the freedom to express oneself. It helps me in my quest to fill my cup with God's grace and try to live the words I write. It's not easy, but if I listen to what others have to say, I often find a reason to believe. Like the time I spent helping at the soup kitchen and the director was telling the group why Jesus wore a crown of thorns. He said Jesus wore the crown of thorns and shed his blood for our thoughts. I never thought of it that way. The way I treat others and the things I do to others begins with my thoughts. Only I can control my thoughts. Only I can choose right from wrong, and God knows we try.

That was the message of the crown. God knows we are going to have thoughts unbecoming of His Presence-let alone other people. Our thoughts can be deceitful and wicked and shameful on the inside but pure and golden-full of good intensions on the outside.

Why am I talking this way? Because our country is going through a very rough time. It's as if I'm not alone anymore with my problem. It seems there are millions like me. I wonder what they're thinking.

I find this an opportunity for all of us to have a fresh start, to find God and our purpose in life. I have found by asking our Lord for help and believing as best I can and being faithful as best I can. *There is hope.*

Tears may fall, and fears may fill our nights, and prayers may seem unanswered. However, believe in Jesus, knowing He loves you and God is with you. If I just get up and do something of good, maybe I will find that sometimes- *love is in need of love.* As long as I breathe-there will be a need for someone. Let me find it and find my worth.

CHAPTER 8

You're Not Alone

Twelve years later …

> I am the vine you are the branches.
> Whoever remains in Me and with Me in
> him will bear fruit in plenty; for cut off
> from Me you can do nothing. [John 15:5]

These are the words of Jesus that we all look to or turn from. I have tried my best to live up to the word of God. Please forgive me, for it has been twelve years since my *last chapter*, and these are my sins.

I have lived through four presidents—*Bush, Obama, Trump, and Biden*—since chapter 7. Forgive me for the chaos and division I have caused by being an American. I realize now that God's words are for everyday use. I'm guilty for choosing party affiliation differences. I'm guilty for not agreeing with friends and family on political issues that may have long-term consequences. I have been clean and sober now for fourteen *tears—I mean years!* However, there seems to be two more paths to take!

> *Whoever lives in love lives in God and God lives in them.* [1 John 4:16]

That is the path I want to take. I know it's a free choice for me to make, and some choices are more difficult than others. So, how do I love someone when no one loves me at less that is how it feels? I have experienced more hatred and division on social media, to the point where some friends have opted out completely. And my opinions and beliefs have not been the most healing.

Taking this path that Jesus has laid down before us *is narrow and difficult.* "To live in love" are not just beautiful words to say; it is difficult when my mind wants to narrow down who it is I will love. Maybe it's fear of the unknown or fear of whom I conceive as my foe. In any case, I must *"love"* if I want to see the best part of God's plan and who I am. To live up to the words of God—that if I live in love, then God lives in me—is powerful. These words add to the richness of life from within. My inner self is all I have and all I will take with me on this quest to find who I am, and I can only do that by- *loving you.*

Jesus said to them, "Where is your faith? Because of your little faith. For truly I say to you, if you have the faith of a mustard seed, you can say to the mountain, 'Move from here to there, and it will move.' Nothing will be impossible for you" [Matthew 17:20].

Wow, it just makes me wonder, if I trust in the Lord the way I should, can I accomplish the impossible? Can I trust in God like I trust in people- when driving down the road- that they will stop at a red light and go on the green? And when I open a can of tuna- can I trust that it's edible? And can I trust there will always be food in the market- both fruits and vegetables? Can I trust that the people who work the fields to put food on our table and bring electricity, water, and gas are working for our betterment?

I think we all trust more than we realize- especially when trusting God. We trust without ever questioning each breath we take- each blink of our eye- each beat of our heart- and each day the sun rises. There are two paths I can take, and after fourteen years of sobriety, I should be able to recognize the path of destruction, the one Jesus said is wide and full of good intentions. However, in this life, it is not easy to love thy neighbor the right way- from the heart- meaningfully and in the name of Jesus. And in the end, would you agree- how we love one another- is how we will be judged on that final day.

["And in the end, the love you take is
equal to the love you make"
                                    -Paul McCartney"]

I believe we do the things we do because it's pleasurable. To take a deep breath is a pleasure. To take a walk in the park or to a bakery or flower shop is a pleasure. To sit down at the table for dinner is a pleasure- and to spend a day with friends is a pleasure. To get a good night's sleep is a pleasure- and to live a day without pain is an awesome pleasure. And the list goes on- with this gift of life God has given us.

I thank you, Lord, for this blissful creation we have been given. So, where did my addiction come from if life itself is a blissful creation? My life is so far from perfection. I wallow in its corruption- not intentionally but subconsciously not fully aware of all the influences that surround me. In order for me to have the faith of a mustard seed, I must know what the truth is. I can ask God to examine my heart and give to God *the only thing that is mine* -my lust, greed, hate, addictions, anger, and arrogant superiority. I believe there are good people out there who do love the right way and have a healthy respect and love for God and everyone. And I believe, in time, those people will move mountains!

There is more to this narrow and difficult road if I can't forgive others as I have been forgiven. Without forgiving others, I don't think I will go anywhere close to this place we call heaven. For we have been forgiven by the pain and sacrifice of Jesus Christ, but I believe He will only call those who have forgiven others as He has forgiven us. First, I must learn to forgive myself for my addictions, and it was never anyone else's fault for my problems.

What happened to me on this life journey *to end my addictions* is what I did fourteen years ago to find a better life. It started with my commitment and devotion to Jesus Christ. I first started walking to church each day for years, and eventually, I was noticed and became a member of the church community. I went from standing at the back of the church to being invited to become a Eucharistic minister. I accepted their graciousness and went to confession after thirty years. I took the VERITAS classes and went on to assist the priest at Communion time with the congregation. I also helped with the homebound ministry to take Communion to convalescent homes and those unable to attend Mass. I believe Jesus is with me in my commitment to Him, and He changed everything. I am no longer living for myself but have a purpose-*that is to love you.*

During this time, I also worked at the Calvary soup kitchen on Saturdays, because the homeless have a special place in my heart. I came up with a six-point plan to house the homeless and find them the help they may need. I would like to share this idea with you because I believe the more, we share ideas, the more minds there are to develop a solution.

Here it is it begins with a building approximately 23,000-square-foot, two-story building, to house approximately 230 people. That would be approximately 50 square feet per bed (OSHA req.), top floor for sleeping quarters, men on one side with women and children on the other. The bottom floor will be used for offices, a kitchen, a dining area, showers, and a laundry.

The first step would be to register the homeless into the center giving them an identity card and mailbox address so the community can identify and communicate with them. The second step would be hygiene given access to showers and clean clothes. After that the third step would be to show them the dining area and give them the time schedule for meals. The fourth step would be to evaluate them for reasons of their homelessness providing counseling services (runaways, pregnancy, battered, substance abuse, and mental illness etc.). Step five would be sleeping arrangements and assignments. And the final step would be the outreach-programs, vocational training, medical referral and mental treatment.

"We are our brother's keeper" and it's hard to see someone's child, regardless of age, living on the streets. There are many reasons, and homelessness is chronic on the streets of America. Everyone has a story and a journey in time that needs to be listened to, if we can only find a way. Addiction doesn't start overnight. It takes time to develop. We should all reach out. If we find our social drinking and drug use has become drinking and drugging alone, we need to reach out! Worse yet we become belligerent and harmful to others we need to reach

out no one else is going to do it for you. If drug use alters your mental capacity to function reach out to someone, no one will think less of you, ask them for help. There are many places you can go and tell those who will listen you need help. Go to AA or NA meetings. They are free. Go to a rehab, but always keep in mind, no one can do for you what you can't do for yourself. Addiction is considered a disease of both the mind and the body. The body can heal if the mind allows it to. No matter where we go or what we do, we will always hear this same message—to reach out to your higher power - that message is for everyone! In AA, they say, "Call on your higher power, even if it's a doorknob." But we have a God who loves us, and Jesus Christ is more than just a doorknob. He is a patient Friend waiting for us to knock on His door.

Never go through a day without saying, "I love you," even if it's to yourself. After all it starts with you and only you can heal this precious gift of life you have been given. In conclusion, I hope someday to hear from your journey in time, your Time Quest and recovery. Remember, the smallest act of kindness can be the greatest and it all starts with you.

I love you- sweet dreams- and good night…

Printed in the United States
by Baker & Taylor Publisher Services